Grief Etiquette

Grief Etiquette

What To Say & How To Say it

Mary Panico

PALMETTO
PUBLISHING
Charleston, SC
www.PalmettoPublishing.com

Copyright © 2024 by Mary Panico

All rights reserved

No portion of this book may be reproduced, stored in a retrieval system, or transmitted in any form by any means– electronic, mechanical, photocopy, recording, or other– except for brief quotations in printed reviews, without prior permission of the author.

Paperback ISBN: 979-8-8229-5043-6

Grief is the price we pay for love.
— *Queen Elizabeth II*

Contents

Chapter 1: My Story 1

Chapter 2: What Is Grief, and What Is Grief Etiquette? . . . 10

    What Is Grief? *10*

    What Is Grief Etiquette?. *12*

Chapter 3: Common Misconceptions About Grief. 14

    Grief Has a Specific Timeline *15*

    Grief Should Be Gotten Over Quickly *16*

    A Grieving Person Needs to Stay Strong *18*

    A Grieving Person Needs to Stay Busy *19*

    Grief Is the Same for Everyone *20*

Chapter 4: Comforting Words Dos and Don'ts. 21

Chapter 5: How to Support a Grieving Person 28

    Listen With Compassion *29*

    Don't Tell Them How to Grieve. *30*

    Don't Compare Grief. *31*

    Don't Tell the Griever When It's Time to Stop Grieving . . *32*

    Encourage Self-Care *33*

    Think Before You Speak *34*

Chapter 6: What Are Helpful Things That You Can Do? . . . 37

Chapter 7: Show Grace to the Grieving Person. 40

Chapter 8: Check in Often on the Grieving Person 43

Chapter 9: Miscarriage 46

Conclusion: Nurturing Compassion 49

Endnotes 51

Acknowledgments 52

My Story

Death: we all know it's a part of life. Despite hearing tragic stories throughout our lives, we tend to believe ourselves immune to its grasp. As we listen to heartbreaking stories, a subtle sense of relief washes over us, quietly relieved that such suffering has not touched our own lives. Then the day comes for us: death arrives at our door with all its ugliness, and our whole lives are forever changed.

For me, the year 2022 began like most other years, full of promise and new adventures on the horizon. I had just completed my postpartum doula training and couldn't wait to get started supporting new mammas and their babies. Little did I know that January this year would bring about tragedy upon tragedy, heartbreak upon heartbreak. The previous month had ended painfully for my extended family. My aunt

Donna, my mom's sister, passed away from pancreatic cancer at the age of fifty-nine after a very short battle. She had only been diagnosed three months before her passing, her decline swift and unexpected.

I remember my mom telling me the news. She was trying to be strong, but I could tell she was in shock. My aunt Donna was one of her closest sisters and had done so much for my family. She had a heart of gold and would give you the shirt off her back in an instant. My sister Gabbie and I flew up to New York for the funeral, trying to support and comfort our mom the best we could.

Going to our aunt's funeral was so surreal. Christmas was just a few weeks away, and there we all were gathered together mourning this great and unexpected loss. Losing our aunt was the first time I'd encountered grief. I knew of people who had passed away, of course, but no one so close to us. My heart broke as I watched my cousins stand at the front of the funeral home, bravely thanking everyone who came to pay their last respects to their mom. I couldn't begin to comprehend their pain in losing a beloved mother so young and unexpectedly. Whoever would have guessed that my mom was about to follow her sister to the grave just a few short months later? That it would soon be my siblings and me who would have to stand in that never-ending line, greeting and thanking everyone who came. Our beautiful mother, who was only fifty-six years old.

My mom called me the day after Christmas wondering if she had caught COVID-19 again. Having just battled it the previous November, she woke up feeling sick once more. As the next couple of weeks passed, she wondered if maybe she had long-term COVID because her symptoms weren't improving, her pain and exhaustion only worsening. My siblings and I never suspected in the least that something terrible was going on. Our mom had always been in good health, focusing on eating healthy and staying in shape. She rarely got sick. The next month was a series of doctor's appointments, and then the dreaded phone call came that confirmed our worst fears. My mom had Stage 4 ovarian cancer, and it had spread throughout her whole body. A thirty-second phone call that shattered our whole world. Words cannot even describe the shock and the utter disbelief that we all felt. How quickly life can change in an instant!

Those first few days after that dreaded phone call were all a blur. I was in total and complete shock. All I could think was: How? How could this be happening? My mom was only fifty-six years old, with so many years ahead of her. I was going to lose one of the most important people in my life. How does one go about preparing oneself for it? My mom, my best friend, who was always there for me. She was the one whom I always went to for advice, with questions, and to share everything and anything. I was only thirty-two; I wasn't supposed to lose her so suddenly and without warning.

I assumed she would be here for at least another twenty or thirty years. She was supposed to see my kids grow up; see them graduate, get married, and so on.

A week after my mom's diagnosis, I bought a one-way ticket up to New York. I felt horrible leaving my two boys, not knowing exactly how long I would be away. My initial thought was to stay for two weeks. That even though she was at Stage 4, she would maybe still be with us for awhile yet. I could get her situated with the best care possible, and then I could return home for a bit. As soon as I saw my mom on my arrival, I knew in an instant that she did not have much time left. How quickly she had deteriorated from the last time I had seen her a mere two months ago. She was all skin and bones. My brain went into power mode. There was no time for grief or to dwell on self-pity. I had to be strong and positive for her sake. My mom needed me to care for her, to help ease her suffering to the best of my ability. We set her up with hospice right away, and I was able to care for her in the comfort of her own home.

Five short weeks was all it took. Five excruciating weeks of seeing her suffer, watching her slip away, the hours of just waiting and wondering when the end would come. Family and friends came to say goodbye; many decisions regarding funeral arrangements had to be made. It was the hardest thing I've ever had to do in my life. My mom was dying, and I was powerless to stop it. My prayers quickly shifted from asking God to heal her to asking that He take her soon, for her suffering to be over. My husband, who was a saint by holding down the fort back home, wondered if I should come home by the third week. I remember being so torn, missing my little boys and husband so much but also knowing that my mom could go at any time. As hard as it was, I knew I had to stay.

We reached a point where I could no longer manage my mom's pain at home, and with a heavy heart, I made the difficult decision to send her to the hospital, where I knew she would receive the expert care she needed. It was especially painful because the hospital had implemented a strict rule allowing only two visitors due to COVID restrictions, and considering my large family, I could only pick one other person to send in. My mom passed away a few days later on March 10 early in the morning. I was numb to the phone call from the nurse at the hospital. My mom's pain and suffering were all over after a very intense and short fight. My husband flew up immediately to be with me, funeral arrangements had all been made, and I had to just somehow get through the next few days. On a cold, wintry day, we laid our beautiful mother to rest. I'll never forget that day as long as I live. I was completely drained both physically and emotionally. I felt only numbness, which in retrospect was a good thing as it helped me to endure the wake, funeral, and burial.

A day later I tearfully said goodbye to my grandmother, wondering if that would be the last time I would see her. My grandma had been fighting cancer as well for the past eight years and was feeling poorly herself. It was heartbreaking to see her sorrow as she had to bury two beloved daughters within three months of each other. Then it was all over, and I was finally heading home to my boys whom I couldn't wait to see. I knew that once I returned, grief would hit me like a thousand bricks, and oh, did it ever. Life was so bleak and empty with one thought ever-present: How do I go through life now without my mamma?

I had only been home a week when I was asked to babysit a friend's children. This friend and her husband had just received some upsetting news regarding a job situation and asked if I would mind giving them a date night so they could get their minds off this disappointment. I had just gotten home after being away from my family for five weeks; I had just buried my young mother, but somehow they felt as though it was all right to ask.

"*We are grieving too*", I was told.

In the weeks that followed, a wave of insensitive comments swept in. I knew people were trying to be supportive and that everyone meant well, but it was shocking to hear certain ones.

"I'm so sorry, but you know, we all have to lose our moms eventually."

"At least you had your mom until you were thirty-two."

"At least you had time to say goodbye to her."

"Look at all the people who die suddenly in car accidents; at least that wasn't your case."

"This person can be your mom now."

Death makes people feel awkward, and I completely understand that people do not quite know what to say. It seems, however, that certain comments should automatically be recognized as ones best left unsaid. I reached out to several friends who I knew had lost a parent as well to ask them if it was just me or if they had received similar comments? They all agreed, saying that, yes, they received all sorts of crazy comments.

Six months after my mom's passing, my siblings and I flew to Michigan for our brother Matt's wedding. After months of grief, we finally had a reason to smile and celebrate as Matt and Valerie pledged their lives to one another. My brother had a condition that runs in our family called hereditary hemorrhagic telangiectasia, a genetic vascular disorder that affects the formation of blood vessels. The previous spring he had been dealing with complications from this disorder, giving us all concern, but we had assumed he would be fine. By the time the wedding came, Matt looked healthy and handsome in his suit as he said his vows at the altar. Both Matt and Valerie were brimming with happiness. What a beautiful, joy-filled day their wedding was! We were all together, celebrating the union of our two families. The deep fog of grief was starting to lift, but then tragedy struck our family once again.

A mere six days later, Matt died while on his honeymoon. An aneurysm had burst, and his heart gave out. I do not even have the words to convey this horror, the unimaginable disbelief that we all felt. We were all just dancing at his wedding, and now we had to make plans for his funeral. How did that even happen? A marriage followed by a funeral, back-to-back. We were still grieving our mom, and now the process started all over again. Grief stacked upon grief.

After Matt's death my siblings and l received continuous, hurtful comments from well-meaning people just like when after our mom died. That there must have been a reason, how our lives were so horrible, and so on. It has been mind-blowing as to what people have said!

We ended 2022 with one more loss. We had received news that my grandma was in her last stages of life, and she passed a month later. My aunt, my mom, my brother, and then my grandma. Four heartbreaking losses in a little over a year. I was torn about flying up for my grandma's funeral. As much as I would have loved to go and give my support to everyone, I ultimately decided not to go. I had been to three funerals in one year, and I knew I could not emotionally handle another one.

***

My Story

Writing a book on grief etiquette has been something on my heart after all my losses. I want to share the dos and don'ts when it comes to supporting those after a loss. I want there to be more of an awareness of what is acceptable to say versus what is not when approaching the grieving person. It is essential for grieving people to not only have support, but to have the *right* kind of support. The wrong kind of support hinders the whole grieving process, but supporting a person the right way is so very crucial and brings about healing.

In this book you will find practical guidance and advice on how to support those who are grieving —whether that person is a family member, a friend, a coworker, or an acquaintance— in a compassionate, loving way. Grief is a universal human experience, and grief etiquette applies to all. Throughout this book, I will share examples from the individuals I've spoken to over the past two years about their experiences with grief. These stories will illustrate how the wrong words and actions can inadvertently cause additional pain. My hope in writing this is to promote more empathy, understanding, and compassion when it comes to grief, and to break down the walls of this subject that is unfortunately taboo in our society. I want to help reduce the social awkwardness that many people feel when they approach a grieving person.

What Is Grief, and What Is Grief Etiquette?

What Is Grief?

Grief is a heart shattered by the weight of loss, a testament to the profound depth of human emotion. It is an intricate tapestry of emotions woven from the threads of sorrow, longing, and remembrance. Grief isn't just about missing someone—it's about grappling with the gaping hole they've left behind, trying to navigate a world that suddenly feels unfamiliar and empty. Grief is a rollercoaster of emotions; it's not just about sadness. It includes anger, guilt, bitterness, loneliness, anxiety, fear, and longing as well. Think of grief as losing an arm or a leg; it is a lifelong journey of learning to live and cope without it.

In 1969 Swiss psychiatrist Elizabeth Kubler-Ross introduced her theory of the five stages of grief in her book *On Death and Dying:* [i]

1. Denial: The disbelief that the loved one is gone. One may act completely normal as if nothing has changed. It is hard to accept the reality of the loss leading to a state of shock and numbness.
2. Anger: As the reality of the loss sets in, anger follows. It can be directed toward oneself, at others, or at the situation. Anger is a defense mechanism that helps one to feel in control and to ignore the pain that they are in.
3. Bargaining: The struggle to understand the loss. The belief is that when we make deals with ourselves or with God, then we will start to feel better. Guilt and irrational thoughts are common during this stage. Examples include: "I'll give up smoking if I can only start to feel better," or "I'll start doing X if only God will bring this person back." It is a state of thought of "If I do this, then that will happen."
4. Depression: A constant feeling of sadness and loss of interest in life. Symptoms can range from loss of appetite, insomnia, and fatigue to lack of concentration, isolation, and hopelessness.
5. Acceptance: Accepting the reality of the loss. It doesn't mean that one has moved on, but that one has learned how to live with the loss.

Some studies show that grief has a profound effect on our brains.[ii] The brain interprets grief as emotional trauma or PTSD. As a result, our brains turn on the fight-or-flight mechanisms, causing our blood pressure and heart rates to increase. One is overloaded with thoughts of sadness, guilt, loneliness, and many other emotions. We call this the "Grief Brain," which affects our memory, concentration, and cognition. This all-consuming state of mind makes it hard to focus on everyday tasks. One may become very forgetful; easy decisions may now seem daunting. It may seem as if the person is completely in a fog. This is all a natural part of grief that is only temporary. It does subside with time.

What Is Grief Etiquette?

When we think of the word 'etiquette', polite manners and social norms come to mind. It is a set of rules and guidelines that tell us how to act in certain situations. We have etiquette guidelines for weddings, job interviews, social events, and more. When it comes to grief, however, there is very little guidance available on how to act or what to say. But just as weddings, for example, require the proper etiquette, so grief requires the same. Grief etiquette teaches us how to express empathy, sensitivity, and genuine loving care for those who are grieving. It is the delicate dance of compassion where our words and gestures express support without intrusion and understanding without judgment. Grief etiquette fosters an environment of connection and healing in the lives of those who are grieving, allowing them to feel heard, supported, and validated.

Common Misconceptions About Grief

There are popular misconceptions about grief in our society that only make the grieving process harder, causing frustration and hurt to the griever.

Five of the most common ones are:

- Grief has a specific timeline.
- Grief should be gotten over quickly.
- A grieving person needs to be strong.
- A grieving person needs to stay busy.
- Grief is the same for everyone.

These are all false as I will show.

Grief Has a Specific Timeline

Often people assume that grief is a set timeframe that one has to go through, and by point "X," it is over, and now you will be fine. How I wish it were that simple! Grief is neither predictable nor orderly. One cannot fit it into neat little boxes.

Comments such as "time heals all wounds" are often said to a griever, but grief doesn't have an expiration date. One wouldn't tell the man who just lost his leg, "Oh, you'll be fine without your leg in a little while." Imagine the shock that people would have if they heard such a comment! Yet grieving people are told constantly that time will help them and that they will be fine in a certain amount of time. However, grief lasts a lifetime because we will always love the person who has died. One learns how to live with a loss, but the pain never goes away completely. The phrase "time heals all wounds" is better used in the context of a breakup or a job loss rather than in the loss of a loved one.

Contrary to common belief, the five stages of grief that we talked about in the previous chapter do not always come in a linear order. One may go through all these stages or only some of them. Some people may experience the same stage twice. There is no hardest stage, as grief is so vastly different from person to person. Some will say that the first year of grief is the hardest, but that isn't always true. The second year can be just as painful, if not harder, for many. People in grief can bounce around between all the various thoughts and emotions that arise from these stages. One can go from soothing thoughts, "They had a great life," to troubling ones, "It wasn't their time to go yet." They can bounce from thoughts of "There wasn't anything I could have done" to the guilty "What if I could have done something? Maybe it is my fault."

Grief is unpredictable; strong emotions can emerge seemingly from nowhere, hijacking any given moment. Two months after my mom died, I was having a good day, feeling positive and like myself. I went to my local botanical gardens and was enjoying my time there when a mother and daughter came up to me and asked if I would mind taking their picture. Tears immediately sprung to my eyes, and I quickly snapped a picture, fighting back my tears. What began as a peaceful day concluded with me in a puddle of tears. Seemingly mundane triggers can bring about intense emotions. One may be out shopping at the grocery store, and all it takes is hearing their loved one's favorite song playing on the radio to quickly bring them to their knees.

In recognizing that grief knows no timetable, we must offer those who are grieving the patience and understanding needed to navigate its unpredictable course.

Grief Should Be Gotten Over Quickly

Dr Megan Shen, a grief expert and associate professor at Fred Hutchinson Cancer Center says, "Culturally, America is a terrible place to grieve. American culture and infrastructure devalue and fail to provide the resources, space, time, and normalization needed to grieve." [iii] Roughly 2.5 million people die in America each year,[iv] leaving behind on average five grieving loved ones. That makes at least 12.5 million grieving individuals a year. Yet most corporate businesses give employees the typical three days of bereavement. That's it. People are expected to go back to normal shortly after a loss. Grief is seen as something to be overcome instead of experienced. The result is that many grieve in isolation or attempt to ignore it.

American culture places a strong emphasis on positive thinking and wellness routines, with abundant resources available on healthy living, exercise, and similar topics. However, discussions on grief and death are often ignored and stigmatized. According to Dr. Shen, there's a glaring lack of open dialogue on how to support grieving individuals.

It is reported that 68 percent of Americans would like to see a change regarding this—more open conversations around grief. Unlike Eastern cultures where death is viewed as part of life, Western society tends to approach it with apprehension and resistance, resulting in heightened anxiety.[v] Doing my research, I was very surprised to learn that in Egypt, it is normal and expected to grieve for seven years after a loss, whereas in the United States, grieving for more than twelve months is labeled as a 'prolonged grief disorder'. Despite the common occurrence of grief and loss, these topics remain taboo in our society. It begs the question: why are they considered such taboo subjects when they are such universal experiences? It's clear that our society must reevaluate its approach to these vital topics.

A Grieving Person Needs to Stay Strong

After losing someone, many people are advised to stay strong or try to stay positive. They are common sayings from those with good intentions, but such phrases can be very hard for a griever to hear. A grieving person feels the complete opposite of strong, and hearing such statements can make them feel patronized and misunderstood. Being told to stay strong comes across almost as a challenge that they have to hold it together or there will be consequences. Comments such as "tears won't bring him back" or "they wouldn't want you to cry" only hinder the grieving process. Tears are not a sign of weakness; they are nature's way of releasing internal tension in the body, providing emotional and physical relief.

This aligns with what we just discussed; we live in a death-denying society where there's always a silent pressure not to express any emotions, leaving the grieving person feeling like they have to put on a mask to the outside world. A new burden is now placed on the griever, resulting in internal anxiety and confusion for them. For me, no one said outright that I had to be strong for my kids' sake after my losses. It was something more implied, that I shouldn't cry or grieve in front of them. I felt the silent pressure to always be strong. The best advice I received was that it is perfectly all right for our kids (or anyone!) to see us grieve. It truly is sad that we often feel like we need permission to grieve. Whenever I had a moment in front of my boys, their reaction was always so comforting. They would run up to me with the biggest hugs, telling me everything would be okay and saying how much they also missed their grandma and uncle. Kids are resilient, and they can handle seeing our emotions.

It's important to encourage the griever to feel all their emotions. Let them know that it's okay to cry or vent when they need to, and that they don't have to ignore or suppress their feelings.

A Grieving Person Needs to Stay Busy

Grief is like a terrible wound that needs medical attention. The longer you ignore it, the more that wound is going to fester, resulting in more destruction down the road. It's the same with grief; it must be experienced, not ignored, in order to heal.

Grieving people are often told that they need to just stay busy, but that is counterproductive. Ignoring grief does more damage in the long run. A broken heart cannot be ignored. One has to do the grief work just like someone with a physical wound has to go to the doctor to get medical treatment. Grief is a natural process that needs to be felt and processed.

Avoiding grief only leads to negative consequences, including physical problems, anxiety, and depression.

Grief Is the Same for Everyone

Each person's grief is as unique as their fingerprints, shaped by a multitude of factors such as the circumstances of the death, the griever's personality and religious background. No two individuals experience the same grief journey. After a loss, everyone responds differently. Some start grieving right away, while others feel numb or shocked and may not begin the process for a while. Coping mechanisms vary greatly- some carry on with their normal lives, while others need time alone. Some will want to be around people, others won't. For some, daily life might continue unchanged, while for others, the simplest tasks may become overwhelming. What helped one person in their grief may not necessarily help another. There's no one 'correct' way to grieve.

Comforting Words Dos and Don'ts

There are many platitudes and clichés that are said so often to a grieving person that can hinder rather than help. Although these common sayings are meant to offer comfort, they can minimize the griever's pain and can become hurdles to their healing. In this chapter we will explore the dos and don'ts of offering comfort through words.

*Do s*ay:

"I'm so sorry for your loss. I'm here for you."

I have found in my grief that the most comforting words from people were "Mary, I'm here." Three short words but so meaningful. To know that people were there whether it was a 1:00 a.m. phone call I needed to make when I couldn't sleep or knowing they would rush over in an instant if I asked them to.

People often feel the need to say more, but a short and heartfelt message is more than enough. It conveys both condolences and support. For me, it was hard to hear when some people rambled on or tried to explain why my losses must have happened.

Here are some other compassionate phrases to say:

- "You are not alone."
- "You are loved, and we are right here."
- "No matter what, we will walk beside you."
- "You are in our thoughts and prayers."
- "Heartfelt condolences on your loved one's passing. May their memory bring you comfort."
- "You have our deepest sympathies."

On the other hand, *don't* be silent. Saying nothing at all to the grieving person can be just as hurtful. Sometimes people will dodge the grieving person due to them being uncomfortable or unsure of what to say. I know of someone who told me that after she lost her mom, two of her lifelong friends didn't say a word of condolence to her. They had known her mom very well but didn't utter one word of sympathy; they completely ignored it, which was painful for her. It's so important to acknowledge the loss but to keep it short and simple.

Don't say:

"Let me know if there's anything I can do." While this statement is not necessarily wrong, it can come across as trite and places the burden on the griever. A grieving person lacks the clarity and energy to even know what it is that they need or want.

Instead *do* offer specific help. Some examples could be:

"I am going to make you a meal. Please let me know when the best day would be to drop it off at your front door." Wording it this way takes off the pressure that they have to visit or chat with you if they aren't ready to do so.

"I'm going to come watch your kids on this day so you can have some alone time."

"I will pick up your kids from school for X amount of time."

"I will drop off some groceries on this day."

Don't ask:

"How are you doing?" Most of the time a grieving person does not even know how to answer that question. I know that when people asked me that after my losses, I couldn't help but think, "I just lost a beloved family member; how else would I be but sad?" A grieving person feels like they have to answer positively with the standard "I'm fine," even if they feel anything but.

However, *do* ask specific questions, such as:

"Have you eaten lunch today?"

"How much sleep have you gotten?"

"What does your grief look like these days?" This question reassures the griever that what they are feeling is normal and allows them to talk about it if they need to.

A friend of mine told me that after losing her dad, her favorite question she had ever been asked was, "How is your heart?"

Don't tell the grieving person: "I know how you feel," as it comes across as dismissive. A griever is in the worst pain imaginable and cannot fathom that anyone truly understands how they feel. Even if you have experienced a loss, everyone feels so differently. A better phrase that shows empathy is: "I can't possibly understand how you feel or what you are going through."

Don't ask how the person died, at least not initially. Asking a grieving person "What happened?" or "How did they die?" can be intrusive. If they want to share that information, they will do so in their own time. While it's natural to be curious, it's important to remember that these questions can cause pain. After my brother died, it was hurtful when people I barely knew or talked to asked these types of questions. Such inquiries often stem from curiosity rather than genuine sympathy. My sister had a similar experience when coworkers at her new job questioned her about his death without offering any condolences. These questions can add to the already heavy burden of grief.

Don't say:

"Everything happens for a reason." This is an all too common platitude that many grievers constantly hear, yet it offers no comfort. It can make the grieving person feel as though their suffering is somehow justified or necessary for a greater purpose. It overlooks and invalidates their pain, often causing the griever to feel anger and frustration. My siblings and I were often told how lucky our mom and brother were for leaving this world, that their sufferings were over. And while we all have our strong faith and belief in the afterlife, hearing such statements in our early days of grief was not in the least bit helpful.

Do talk about the deceased person.

A lot of times, people supporting the grieving person will avoid saying the deceased person's name. They will awkwardly avoid all mention of them as they worry it will bring them pain. Please don't do this; a grieving person is constantly thinking about their loved one; they want to hear all about them. They may not be with us anymore, but they do not cease to be. We want to keep their memories very much alive, to know that they are not forgotten. Encourage the griever to talk about the one they have lost. If you knew the deceased person well, tell them what they meant to you. How did they impact your life? What was it that you loved most about them? What is your favorite memory of them? Share a funny story of them, a touching scene and so on.

After my losses I loved when friends and family shared with me their favorite stories of them, hearing how they helped so many others, hearing all the different stories. They were a balm to my hurt; they lifted me and brought a smile to my face.

If you never knew the person, then encourage them to tell you all about them. Ask them what their name is. What were they like? What is your best memory of them? It is so therapeutic to just talk about our loved ones, to hear all about them. To share pictures, stories, and so on.

Speaking of them brings about healing and comfort. This may sound silly, but when I would share pictures of my mom with those who never knew her, I loved it when people spoke of her in the present tense versus the past. Comments like "Your mom is beautiful" instead of "She was beautiful."

Don't start a sentence with "at least."

This saying happens all too frequently, in a variety of ways, but it's one of the worst things a griever can hear. It suggests a positive aspect to the loss where there is none. Comments such as these are often said:

"At least they are in a better place."

"At least you still have this person."

"At least they lived a long life."

"At least they are not suffering anymore."

"At least you were able to say goodbye."

While many of these statements can hold truth, it doesn't mean they are helpful or comforting. There are no silver linings to a loss and these types of comments only minimize the deep pain that the grieving person is in.

One of my friends lost her father as a child and shared with me how painful it still is to hear people say, "At least you lost him while you were so young." These comments only diminish the significance of her loss and wrongly assume that her grief would be less if she had lost him as an adult. She was deprived of a father growing up and never had the chance to create the memories that other children have with their fathers. Perhaps it would have been less painful if she had lost him later in life.

On the flip side, when an older person dies, people often say to the griever, "At least they lived a long life" or "At least you had them for so many years." However, grief knows no age or time limit. Heartbreak remains heartbreak, irrespective of the circumstances. Regardless of age, the grieving person feels like that life wasn't long enough. Whether one is five, fifteen, or ninety-five, pain remains pain.

How to Support a Grieving Person

When someone we care about is hurting, it's only natural to want to ease their pain. Whether they've lost a parent, a spouse, a child, or a friend, life is now drastically different for them. However, the reality is that you can't "fix" their grief. As much as you would like to, you can't take away their pain, but you can be beside them while they hurt. There are no magical words you can say to make them feel better about their loss, but there are things you can do that provide comfort and support. As they navigate the storms of grief, you can show them that they are not alone in their pain.

Listen With Compassion

More often than not, your presence speaks louder than words. This is a time to walk along with the griever silently, picking up the pieces for them while they crumble and don't know what pieces they have left. Often people feel the need to fill the silence with unnecessary talk, but it can make the grieving person uncomfortable. Please remember that you don't need to have all the perfect words or have to give the right advice. Sometimes, the greatest comfort comes from shared silence, where words are unnecessary.

The day my brother died, two friends of mine rushed over that night and just sat with me, listening as I cried out my shock and disbelief. They didn't need to say much; it was comforting to just have them present with me.

A friend of ours recently lost his sister-in-law to a sudden illness. His brother said that what he appreciated the most was when a friend came over with a book, saying, "I'll be here all day. I'm here if you need to talk, but if not, that is okay too."

Please listen more than you speak. Encourage the griever to share their feelings and thoughts without providing solutions or answers. If they are not ready or willing to talk, then please don't push them. They will open up if and when they are ready. You can encourage them to journal; there is a lot of comfort in writing down all the different thoughts and feelings that grief brings about. If they ask for advice, then by all means, you can suggest things like finding a good therapist or finding a grief support group. But if they don't ask for advice, then please refrain from offering it. You may have the best intentions to help, but it won't come across as such to them. Hug them, sit with them—your presence alone is a source of comfort.

Don't Tell Them How to Grieve
Remember that there is no one-size-fits-all approach to grieving, and that everyone experiences it differently. Grieving people are often met with strong opinions about what they should or shouldn't do and what will or won't help them. While these opinions are well intended, instead of helping, they just aggravate the griever. Even if you've experienced grief yourself, please refrain from giving advice. What helped you in your grief doesn't necessarily mean that it will help them. This is about their journey, not yours. Always follow their lead by listening to their cues. Sometimes they may not know what they want, and that is perfectly all right. Please respect their needs and boundaries by allowing them to grieve in their own way. Your role is to offer comfort, not judgment.

A person in the midst of grief is so vulnerable, and their emotions are all over the place. Please don't give them more emotional work to do. Reassure them that their thoughts and feelings are normal and valid and that you are there for them without judgment or criticism. A lot of people who have experienced grief have said, years later, they wished someone had reassured them that they were not going crazy in their early days of grief. A phrase like, "It's okay to feel whatever you're feeling right now" can be incredibly helpful for a griever to hear.

Don't Compare Grief

Relationships are all different. The loss of a spouse is different from the loss of a parent. The loss of a child is different from the loss of a friend. No two people are the same, and no two losses are the same. Everyone's grief is tailored uniquely to them.

My therapist shared with me that a few months after she lost her mom, her friend lost her cat and told her that now she understands what grief is and what it was that she went through. Pet grief is real, of course, but to place it on the same level as losing a parent is ludicrous!

I was flabbergasted when a friend of mine compared the death of my mom to her husband's job situation by saying, "I know it's not the same, but you obviously understand grief. I'm crying all day too."

Another person shared with me that after her mom's death, she was told, "I know it's been only a few months, but you have to keep things in perspective and appreciate life. My friend had back surgery and can no longer walk." I'm certain that anyone who has lost a loved one would agree: they would prefer to have their loved one in a wheelchair than no longer here with them!

It is useless to compare grief. Knowing someone else has it 'worse' does not diminish the severity of the griever's pain or make their loss any less significant. Pain is incomparable.

Don't Tell the Griever When It's Time to Stop Grieving

About six months after my mom passed, a friend came over while I was having a moment. He was surprised that I still had my hard days, remarking that I wasn't a child and that I needed to toughen up and move on.

Please do not tell a person when it's time to stop grieving. It shows a complete lack of empathy and isn't really anyone's place to decide. As we have said before, there is no expiration date when it comes to grief. All too often grieving people are met with the following types of comments:

"How long are you going to be sad for?"

"I want the old you back."

"You're not the same person anymore."

"You're always sad now."

There is often a silent pressure from friends and family to move on, that the time for grief has passed. However, grief changes a person entirely, and these types of comments only add to their burden. More than likely, they won't ever completely return to the way they used to be. Grief leaves an indelible mark, and life is so different now for them. Pressuring someone to move on or suggesting they've grieved for too long can cause resentment, hindering their healing journey and pushing the griever into a state of isolation.

I recently had a client who shared with me that she had lost her mom a decade ago. When I asked her how she was doing, she started crying, saying that no one ever asks her that anymore. While it is true that grief can ease over time, the pain of a loss will always be there, whether it's been one year or fifty years.

Others have shared with me that when they mention losing their loved ones over five years ago, they are often met with very little sympathy. It's as if society expects the passage of time to erase their pain. I know that my mom and brother's deaths will always be a deep sadness for me. I'll never stop grieving them. There will always be an ache there inside, and I will still have my share of hard days.

Encourage Self-Care

Grief is exhausting and drains one completely. Self-care plays a crucial role in the healing journey. When supporting one in grief, make sure they have enough food and are drinking enough water. Encourage them to take long naps, to get plenty of rest. Sad dreams and nightmares can be common right after a loss. My sleep was very disturbed for awhile after I lost my mom and then again after I lost my brother. By prioritizing self-care, a grieving person can replenish their energy, allowing them to navigate their grief with greater resilience.

After a loss, it's common for a grieving person to feel guilt, whether it's from the belief that they could have prevented the loss or from the burden of survivor's guilt. It's normal for them to feel like they can't smile, laugh, or enjoy life anymore, believing it to be disrespectful to the one they have lost. Encourage them that it's perfectly all right to take a break from grieving. Remind them that there's nothing wrong with going out and doing something fun to get their minds off of it for a little bit. Taking moments to enjoy life doesn't mean they have moved on or have forgotten their loved one. They provide much-needed relief and respite, which is an essential part of the healing process.

Think Before You Speak

Words are powerful and have such a profound impact on a grieving person. When words are necessary, they should be chosen with care and consideration. The best intentions will not negate a hurtful comment and can sting even years later. A good rule of thumb is: if you're not sure if something should be said, then please don't say it. A grieving person has heightened sensitivity, so it is far better to err on the side of caution.

The following stories shared with me will illustrate how the wrong words can be incredibly damaging and hurtful to someone in the throes of grief, emphasizing why grief etiquette is much needed.

Katie was at a New Year's Eve party one week after her mom's passing, and when a relative noticed she wasn't partying, he asked in surprise, "She's not over it yet?" Asking after a year would have been insensitive enough, let alone seven short days!

Sarah's mom died right before COVID-19 hit and was asked by a friend, "Aren't you happy that your mom died before COVID?" How can the word *happy* go in the same sentence as *died*?

A day after her mom died of cancer, Anna's friend told her, "I told you to give your mom a dog-wormer to get rid of the cancer, but because you didn't listen, it's your fault she died."

After telling a lady that her mom just died, Kara was told, "I'm praying for you…I am so glad that I still have my mom; these are all the plans that she has for me."

When Alex returned to work after her mom's passing, her coworker asked her, "Are you all better now?" followed by, "You should feel better now that she's not still here and sick."

Brianna was told by a friend, "You have been annoying and not the same since your mom's death."

A lady at church said to Emily, "Your mom's death is for the best; now you can get on with your life."

Bree was told, "You can't just sit around all the time feeling sorry for yourself."

Others have told me that after sharing news of their fathers' deaths, they often get asked, "Were you close with him?" Similarly, another person told me that after her mom's death, she was told, "At least you and your mom weren't close." The intensity of grief does not depend on how close or distant the relationship was with the person who passed away. For example, I have another friend who wasn't close with her father, yet when she lost him, her grief was still intense.

I could continue with further stories, but these are more than enough to show how very important tact is when approaching someone who is grieving. It is far better to say nothing than to make outlandish remarks. Insensitive comments will always cause pain, and even though we might convince ourselves that they were well-intentioned, the hurt they inflict can remain.

What Are Helpful Things That You Can Do?

Here are some thoughtful suggestions of what you can do to express your love and support to someone who is grieving:

- Send flowers.
- Send them a meal or start a meal train for them.
- Write a heartfelt sympathy card.
- Offer to babysit their kids so they can have time alone.
- Bring them groceries.
- Bring over coffee in the morning/send their favorite beverage.
- Offer to assist with chores, housework, paying bills for them, etc.

- Donate to the deceased person's favorite charity in their honor.
- Run errands for them.
- Send a personalized gift.
- Send comfort items: a cozy blanket, a candle, a journal, a gift basket, etc.

The day I got the news of my mom's fatal diagnosis, I opened my front door later to find bottles of wine that a friend had sent. Friends sent meals after I lost my mom and my brother, and others set up a meal train for me. It was a huge relief in those early days of grief not to have to worry about cooking for my family, and it eased my burden a little. One of my friends gave me a Willow Tree figure of a mother and daughter hugging right after my mom died. She was worried it might make me cry, but I was so touched by the thoughtful gift. It sits on my dresser now and makes me smile every time I look at it.

I loved it when friends sent me flowers. There's nothing like fresh, beautiful flowers to bring in a little cheer during the dark days of grief. They are a visible reminder of the love and respect for the person who has passed away.

Examples of personalized gifts might include a photo album compiled with their loved one's favorite photos, a quilt made from their clothing, or jewelry engraved with their initials. I love the "Wear Felicity" bracelet and necklaces. They are designed to hold any picture in a small charm, allowing you to see the image of your loved one whenever you hold the charm up to a light. After my brother passed away, some friends gifted me one with a picture of us from our childhood. I loved it so much that I went and ordered a similar one of my mom and me.

I was grateful when someone suggested bringing recordings of my mom's voice to 'Build-A-Bear,' where they can insert them into a stuffed animal. It's very comforting for me to have this little bear, knowing that it holds almost sixty seconds of my mom's voice whenever I press the button.

While these gestures may not seem monumental or feel like they're enough, they truly do provide comfort to someone who is grieving.

Show Grace to the Grieving Person

It's crucial to remember that a grieving person experiences a whirlwind rollercoaster of emotions. It is remarkable how quickly one can transition from sadness to anger to hurt. I remember from the early days of my grief how I could be laughing at something one minute and then crying uncontrollably the next. It is so important to extend grace to those who are grieving; they need your love and support now more than ever.

In an online grief support group I'm a part of, I was shocked to see many women posting about their marriages falling apart because their husbands are angry with them for being so sad all the time. At a time when these women need their husbands' love and support more than ever, they are instead met with anger. Many of these wives were even given an ultimatum: start being happy again or their husbands would leave. As if grief could be simply switched on and off like a light switch!

My husband was my rock during the early days of my grief after I lost my mom, and then again after I lost my brother. In hindsight I realized that during those dark days, I was unintentionally taking out my pain and grief on him. A simple comment from him, remarking that our house was cluttered, would set me off, assuming he was criticizing my ability to keep the house clean, when in fact that was the furthest thing that he had meant! Please know that if the person you are supporting lashes out at you, it's the pain speaking, not them. Please try not to take anything personally.

Extending grace to a grieving person shows compassion, support, validation, comfort, and respect. It demonstrates compassion by acknowledging their pain and offering support in their time of need. It provides validation by recognizing their emotions and experiences as valid and understandable. It offers comfort by creating a safe space for them. And it shows respect by honoring their individual journey during one of the most challenging times in their life.

Always keep this thought in mind: if I were the one going through a loss, how would I want to be treated? As the old saying goes, "Don't judge a man until you've walked a mile in their shoes."

My own experience with grief has taught me the value of treating others with compassion. From the angry sales associate at the store to the rude waitress at that restaurant, and to that coworker who messed up on the project—we don't always know what battles people are silently fighting. Many may be masking their pain with other emotions. It is so important to be kind!

Check in Often on the Grieving Person

Grief is a long, ongoing journey, making your continual support essential. The consensus among everyone I've talked to about grief is that initially, there is an outpouring of support, but as time passes, others return to their routines and assume the grieving person is doing the same. This shift in support can create a sense of abandonment for those still struggling with the loss. Please remember to check in on them regularly, regardless of how much time has passed. A simple text message or a phone call can make a world of difference in letting them know they are not alone in their grief journey.

Grief weighs heaviest during the holidays, birthdays, and especially on the anniversary of a loved one's passing. Despite the world moving forward, the absence of their presence lingers as a stark reminder of the profound loss. These days will always be tinged with sorrow.

I love what Sarah Nannen, a young military widow and grief expert, has to say about grief during the holidays: "If you're inviting someone to your home and they're grieving, be sure that you invite their grief too. It will be there anyway."[vi] She stresses the importance of honoring their needs and emotions. A great way to word an invitation to a holiday party, according to Sarah, is: "I know this season is extra hard, and your heart is hurting. You and your grief are welcome in our home. Come as you are; we would be honored to have you with us." Wording it this way takes off the pressure of having to come in a happy mood. Grieving people often decline social events out of fear that they will feel miserable or unwelcome. It's crucial to communicate to them that they are wanted and accepted just as they are, without needing to pretend. It's also thoughtful to extend invitations without expecting immediate commitments, allowing them the flexibility to change their mind. For instance, saying something like, "You don't have to decide now; it's completely okay if you decide at the last minute" can offer them the freedom to attend if they feel up to it.

To acknowledge the birthdays and death anniversaries of the loved one that the griever has lost, consider hosting a gathering to commemorate their life and legacy. Invite all who knew and loved them to share stories and special moments.

Check in Often on the Grieving Person

Sharing pictures and reminiscing about fond memories can help keep their spirit alive. Similarly, on the anniversary of their death, it's important not to let the griever be alone on this incredibly tough day. Knowing that friends and family are always there for them aids in their healing process. Encouraging them to establish their own rituals on these days can provide a sense of connection and comfort. Despite the physical distance between my mom's grave in New York and my living in Texas, I've found ways to honor her birthday and the anniversary of her death. My mom had such a love for nature and flowers, and her favorite restaurant was Red Lobster. Visiting the botanical gardens and then enjoying a meal at Red Lobster is my way of honoring her memory and feeling close to her by participating in activities that she so loved doing.

9

Miscarriage

I want to include miscarriage in this book because it's a topic that isn't often associated with grief, as it should be. While most people understand the various faces of grief such as the loss of a family member, a spouse, or a friend, miscarriage is often perceived in our society as more of a disappointment rather than another form of grief—the loss of a potential child instead of an actual child.

Miscarriage can be just as devastating as any other loss, and grief etiquette applies here as well. It's a common occurrence today; with studies showing that one in five women will miscarry.[vii] Many women grieve the loss of a beloved child, and their grief is only made worse by others who downplay this or make insensitive remarks.

Following a pregnancy loss, women often encounter a range of hurtful comments, including the following:

"You're young, and you'll have another baby eventually."

"At least you can get pregnant."

"A lot of women go through the same thing."

"At least it happened now and not later."

"It's just not the right timing."

"At least you have other children to focus on."

"There must have been something wrong with the baby."

I know of a mom who lost her baby at birth. She had multiple boys already, and on finding out this was another boy, she was told, "At least it wasn't a girl this time." As if that could possibly bring any comfort! Remember, there are no positives to a loss, no silver linings to be found.

These comments only serve to deepen the mother's grief. No matter the stage of her pregnancy's end, the due date will always be painful for her. Whether she has other children already or not is a moot point. An irreplaceable void is left by this child she will never hold, never hear, never see. She'll always grieve the child that never came to be.

What is the appropriate response to say instead? Just as we've discussed before, "I'm so sorry for your loss, I'm here for you." Just as with any other loss, it's crucial to apply the same etiquette and support here. A mother who has suffered a miscarriage requires the same empathy and compassion as anyone else in the aftermath of a loss. Offer your presence to the mom, actively listen to her, and support her in taking as much time as she needs to grieve. Ensure she has ample time to recover both physically and emotionally. Many women feel guilt after a pregnancy loss, believing they must have done something to cause it. Reassure them that this is not the case, and there is nothing they could have done to prevent it. Encouraging the mom to name her baby is a wonderful way for her to feel connected and keep their memory alive. Additionally suggesting that she choose a special item, such as a Christmas tree ornament, a blanket, or a teddy bear, can provide comfort and serve as a tangible reminder of her precious baby. You could offer further suggestions for memorializing the baby, such as creating a memory box or planting a tree or flower in their honor.

In supporting a woman after a miscarriage, we not only offer comfort in her time of need but also become a crucial part of her healing journey.

Conclusion: Nurturing Compassion

Grief is a universal experience, and none of us is immune to the pain of loss. Grief etiquette is a language of compassion spoken through our actions, words, and presence. It calls upon us to listen compassionately, to speak with sincerity, and to offer comfort with genuine empathy to those who are navigating the storms of grief. As we reflect on the importance of grief etiquette, let us not just simply acknowledge its significance, but instead let us heed a call to action.

We can break the silence surrounding grief by initiating open and honest conversations with friends, family, and colleagues. We can all work together to change the attitudes surrounding death and grief in a positive way. By putting the principles of grief etiquette into action, we can all create a ripple effect of healing and hope in our communities. May our hearts remain open, our ears attuned, and our hands ever ready to comfort. In doing so we can all stand together as beacons of light and love in the darkness of grief, offering hope and healing, knowing that our words and actions have the power to make a profound difference in the lives of those who are grieving.

Endnotes

i   Elizabeth Kubler-Ross, *On Death and Dying* (New York: Macmillan,1969).

ii   Mary-Frances O'Connor, *The Grieving Brain* (New York, 2022).

iii Dr. Megan Shen, *Why It's So Tough to Grieve in America* (*USA Today*, November 28, 2023).

iv Dr. Megan Shen, *Why It's So Tough to Grieve in America* (*USA Today*, November 28, 2023).

v   Dr. Megan Shen, *Why It's So Tough to Grieve in America* (*USA Today*, November 28, 2023).

vi Sarah Nannen, *Holiday Host Etiquette* (*The Well Haven*, December 21, 2021).

vii Miscarriage Association, (2024).

Acknowledgments

After all of my losses, I used to joke that there needs to be a grief etiquette book, but I never imagined that I would be the one to write it. I am deeply grateful to the many individuals who have supported and helped me on this journey.

To my husband, Greg, thank you for your encouragement and for always believing in me, even during the most challenging moments. I could not have done this without you.

To my sisters and friends, your insights and advice have been invaluable throughout this journey, and I am so grateful for all of you.

To the many individuals who have shared their stories with me, thank you for your willingness to open up and share your experiences of grief. They have added depth and richness to this book, and I'm so grateful for you.

To my editor and publishing team at Palmetto, thank you for your expertise and dedication to this project. Your attention to detail and commitment to excellence helped bring this book to life.

Acknowledgments

To my readers, thank you for embarking on this journey with me. Your interest and support are deeply appreciated. Thank you for allowing me to share my insights and experiences with you.

Lastly, I want to extend a special acknowledgment to all those who are experiencing grief. Know that you are not alone on this journey; your presence in this world is cherished, and your journey is honored.

Mary Panico, a devout Catholic from Upstate NY, now resides in Fort Worth, TX with her loving husband, Greg, and their two sons. Her personal experiences with grief have led her to pen her book, *Grief Etiquette: What To Say & How To Say It*. Mary's part-time work as a postpartum doula, assisting new mothers and their babies, is a testament to her compassionate nature. Her faith is her guiding light, and her book aims to help others navigate the universal experience of grief. Mary's words are a beacon of hope and understanding for anyone dealing with loss.

www.ingramcontent.com/pod-product-compliance
Lightning Source LLC
LaVergne TN
LVHW052004060526
838201LV00059B/3830